NEW YORK

NEW

PHOTOGRAPHS BY

FOREWORD BY

YORK

SANTI VISALLI

EDWARD I. KOCH

UNIVERSE

Page 1. The Statue of Liberty
Pages 2–3. Aerial view of the East River, with the Manhattan Bridge
at left and the Brooklyn Bridge at right
Page 5. Wall and Broad streets, the heart of Lower Manhattan

First published in the United States of America in 1995 by
Universe Publishing
A Division of Rizzoli International Publications, Inc.
300 Park Avenue South, New York, NY 10010

95 96 97 98 99 / 10 9 8 7 6 5 4 3 2 1

Library of Congress catalog card number: 95-060813

Design by Gilda Hannah
Printed in Korea

To Gayla, Ivon, and Tony

Edward I. Koch, former Mayor of the City of New York, marching up Fifth Avenue in the 1995 St. Patrick's Day Parade

FOREWORD

EDWARD I. KOCH

When I was asked by Universe to introduce a book that would capture the visual essence of New York City, they mentioned that the photographer, Santi Visalli, and I (with a reputation as, dare I say it, the quintessential New Yorker) would be a wonderful combination. I said, "I'd like to meet him."

Visalli came to my office and brought along slides of his work. He looks like Einstein and talks like Toscanini, and I asked him to tell me a little bit about himself. He came to this country from Sicily in 1959; shortly thereafter, finding no work and running out of money, he was forced to sell his last camera for sixty dollars on MacDougal Street. Clearly, he was not long bereft of the tools of his trade and has since gone on to take over half a million photographs worldwide.

When Visalli showed me the pictures for this book, his genius, humor, and insight came through. He has captured the most famous, as well as the lesser known but still uniquely beautiful, buildings and views of the City of New York. When we speak here of "the City," we mean

Manhattan. Indeed, when traveling to Manhattan, every New York City dweller who lives outside of Manhattan always says, "I'm going to the City." It's a bit like London and that one-square-mile section at its heart, also known as "the City," with its own Lord Mayor.

Out of the dozens of vistas, buildings, exteriors, and interiors that comprise this celebration of New York, I have my favorites and you will have yours. Mine are based on living with these sights for seventy years. Believe me—they have their own life force, and Visalli has captured that spirit.

For me, the most beautiful building in the world is the Chrysler Building. Its Art Deco look still conveys both a mysterious past and a scintillating future. While my attraction to the Chrysler arises from its intrinsic elegance, my second favorite Manhattan building, the Metropolitan Museum of Art, inspires me for its extrinsic value. The building itself is, I am sure, well regarded in architectural circles, but it actually remains unfinished. The granite blocks above the columns at the door, Herodian in their massive girth, have yet to be executed into permanent shape—and, in fact, they never will be, since the building is a landmark and we do not alter landmarks. Rather than appreciating it solely for its physical presence, however, I think of the Met as the world's cultural center, with works spanning ancient and modern, from the pharaohs to Henry Moore. I visit the museum at least twenty-five times a year, to see a new exhibit or to reexperience an old one, and I am never disappointed.

Our artist's photographs take us from north to south and east to west in a journey through the Borough of Manhattan. In one of his frames, Visalli took me back in time to a building where I spent twelve working years: City Hall, pictured with its famous cupola at the top of the clock tower. Topped with a copper figure of Justice, that architectural jewel still gives me a special sense of pride.

I derive a similar pleasure when crossing the Brooklyn Bridge, by car or on foot, glimpsing the bridge towers that were once the tallest structures in New York City. My favorite Visalli photograph of the bridge bathes it in glowing light, its cables forming a spiderweb that captures the City in a beautiful net. The bridge conveys for me the strength and look of the cathedral of Notre Dame. Too overheated you say? Take the trip and see if you don't agree.

Around the tip of the island from the Brooklyn Bridge, Manhattan has a startling satellite city lying within its borders that was begun when I was mayor—Battery Park City. Visalli recalls those early days of construction and also looks ahead to such finished structures as the World Financial Center. While Battery Park City is enormous in occupancy, both commercial and residential, it is not yet completed. It juts out into the Hudson River and, due to the landfill that forms its foundation, stands on the river itself. Its vistas include the World Trade Center and the Statue of Liberty, that symbol of the United States sitting at the entrance to New York Harbor, loved and admired by those who live under her protection and by those who seek it.

All New Yorkers have special attachments to their own neighborhoods—Visalli takes us to Greenwich Village, where I have lived, on lower Fifth Avenue, since leaving Gracie Mansion. His photo of Washington Square Park, which I can see from my apartment's balcony, captures the unique atmosphere that still permeates what was once considered bohemia. You can actually see my apartment building in the background.

So many of Visalli's photographs evoke memories of the special times when I was mayor: Christmas Eve Midnight Mass at St. Patrick's Cathedral, which I still attend at the invitation of John Cardinal O'Connor; the St. Patrick's Day

Parade, in which I continue to march year after year; and the New York City Marathon, for which the incumbent mayor fires the starting cannon. (I have yet to run in the Marathon and doubt I ever will.)

New York City at any time, day or night, is special—sui generis. But building by building, as lovely as our structures are, it would be foolish to say that architecturally we are the most beautiful city in the world. Having traveled to many of the globe's major capitals, I believe Paris deserves that description for its nearly pristine nineteenth-century architecture and the cohesiveness of its design.

What New York has that sets it apart from the truly great cities of the world—Paris, London, Tokyo—is the electricity that comes from diversity. Our buildings vie with one another to be unique. Our people are distinguished by a multitude of origins. We are made up of 175 different races, religions, and ethnic groups. Every nation of the world has sent us its most audacious, intelligent, and entrepreneurial sons and daughters. The entire country prides itself on this unique diversity, but it is through New York City that most of these people first walked upon reaching America's shores.

Being a New Yorker is, as musician Billy Joel sings, a state of mind. Less than fifty percent of the people who live in the City were born here. The other half hails from every part of the world, from every state in the union. I'm one of the few who was born here, and it wasn't in Manhattan, but in the Bronx.

To be a New Yorker does not require citizenship by birth, but rather an acceptance of what this city is all about. It's about architecture, restaurants, museums, Broadway, and people—all are captured by Visalli's lens. We are the capital of so many industries, including commerce, finance, design, fashion, and communications. If you've come here and stayed six months, and you find that you walk faster, talk faster, and think faster, then you're a New Yorker.

Many of those who came to New York left and peopled the other cities and states of this country, but some of the best have stayed behind; each generation has added to the dynamism of New York City. We who continue to live here are the trustees of this great metropolis. Welcome to paradise.

Pages 12–13. Central Park and the Midtown skyline, seen from an Upper West Side penthouse

Page 14. The Chrysler Building (1930), the quintessential Art Deco skyscraper, by William Van Alen

Page 15. The twin towers of the World Trade Center (1973), by Minoru Yamasaki and Emery Roth & Sons; in the foreground is One World Financial Center (1985), by Cesar Pelli

Pages 16–17. Lincoln Center at night, with the New York State Theater (1964), by Philip Johnson, at left, and the Metropolitan Opera House (1966), by Wallace K. Harrison, at right

Page 18. *Globe* (1971), by Fritz Koenig, at the World Trade Center

Page 19. One United Nations Plaza (1976), by Kevin Roche and John Dinkeloo, stands behind the shimmering Nigeria House (1992), near United Nations Headquarters

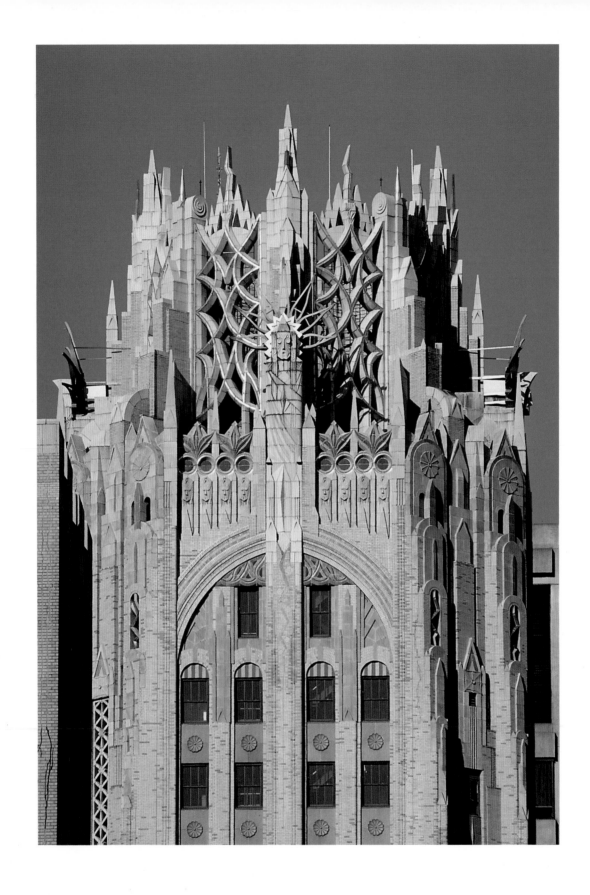

Pages 20–21. The most famous skyline in the world, Lower Manhattan, seen from the Statue of Liberty ferry

Page 22. The top of the General Electric Building (1931), by Cross & Cross, a gem from the era of Art Deco skyscrapers

Page 23. Trinity Church (1846), by Richard Upjohn, once the tallest building in Manhattan, now dwarfed in the canyons of Wall Street

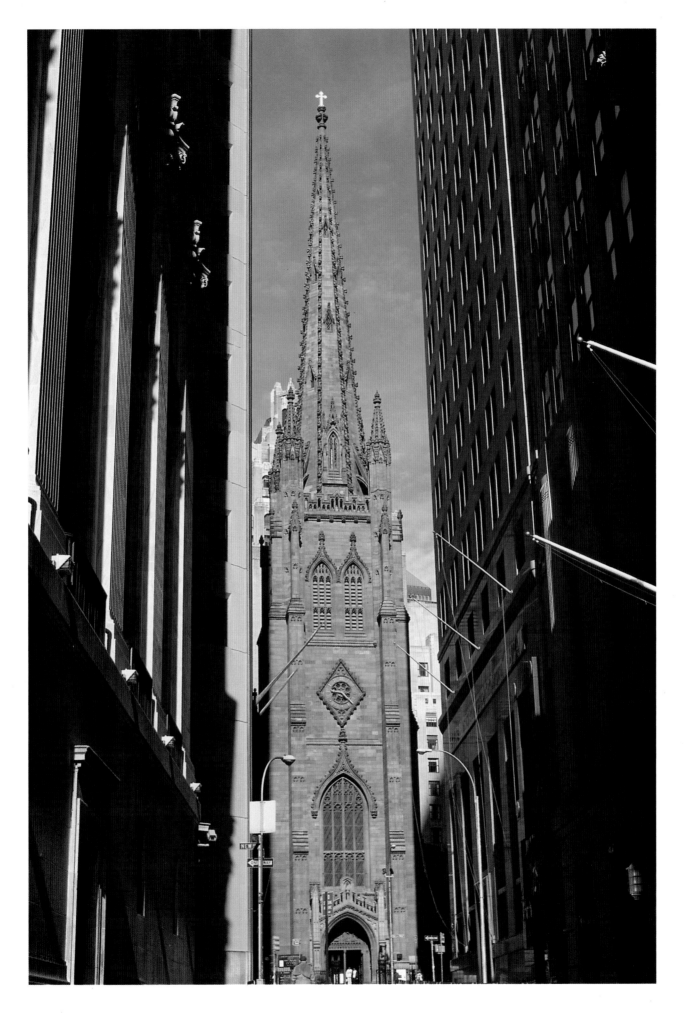

Page 25. The cupola of the Helmsley Building (1929), by Warren and Wetmore, above Park Avenue

Pages 26–27. The grand New York Public Library (1911), by Carrère & Hastings, attracts large lunchtime crowds

Page 28. *George Washington* (1883), by John Quincy Adams Ward, stands watch over the New York Stock Exchange (1903), by George B. Post

Page 29. An outdoor café provides a touch of Paris on Fifth Avenue across from the Plaza Hotel (1907), by Henry J. Hardenbergh

Top. A romantic picnic in Central Park

Bottom. Central Park bicyclists relax in the late afternoon sun

Page 31. The flags of the world fly over Rockefeller Center's summertime café

Pages 32–33. Grand Central Terminal (1903–13), by Reed & Stem and Warren and Wetmore, is the palatial entrance to Manhattan for thousands of commuters

Page 34. The glittering marble-and-brass-filled atrium of Trump Tower (1983), by Der Scutt

Page 35. Gilded highlights, a massive chandelier, and original mosaics grace the lobby of the Waldorf-Astoria Hotel (1931), by Schultze & Weaver

Page 37. Dusk settles on Park Avenue

Pages 38–39. The United Nations Security Council Chamber, with *Peace* (1949), by Per Krogh

Page 40. Palm trees rise ninety feet in the sun-filled Winter Garden (1988), by Cesar Pelli, at the World Financial Center

Page 41. The red granite McGraw-Hill Building (1972), by Harrison, Abramovitz & Harris, soars high above Athelstan Spilhaus's *The Sun Triangle*

Pages 42–43. A winter view of Liberty Island, showcasing the Statue of Liberty's star-shaped base, by Richard Morris Hunt

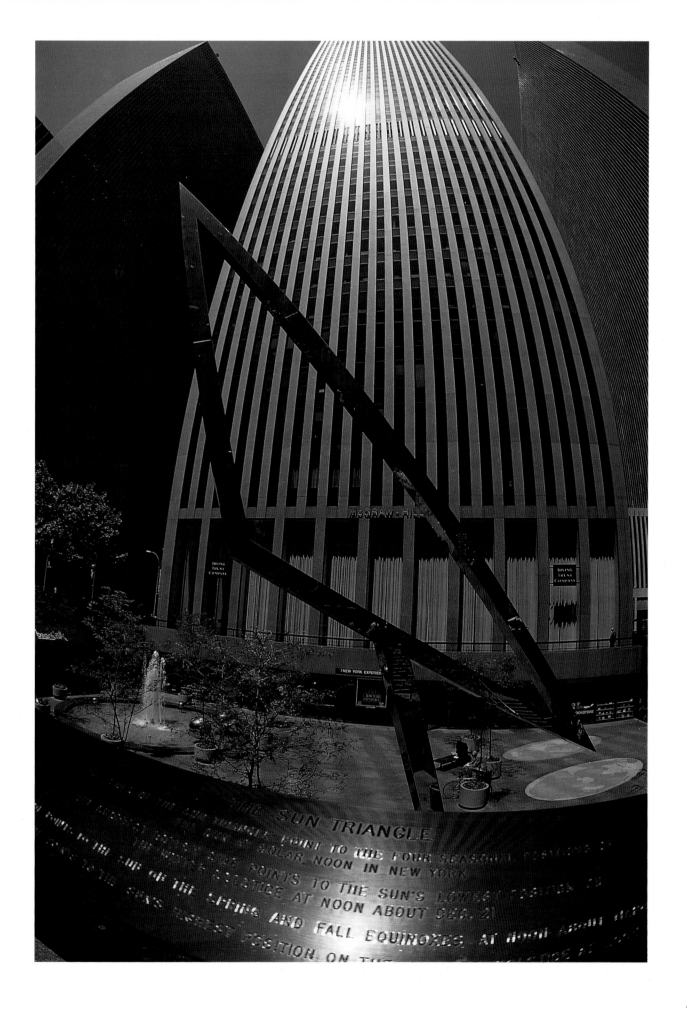

THE SUN TRIANGLE

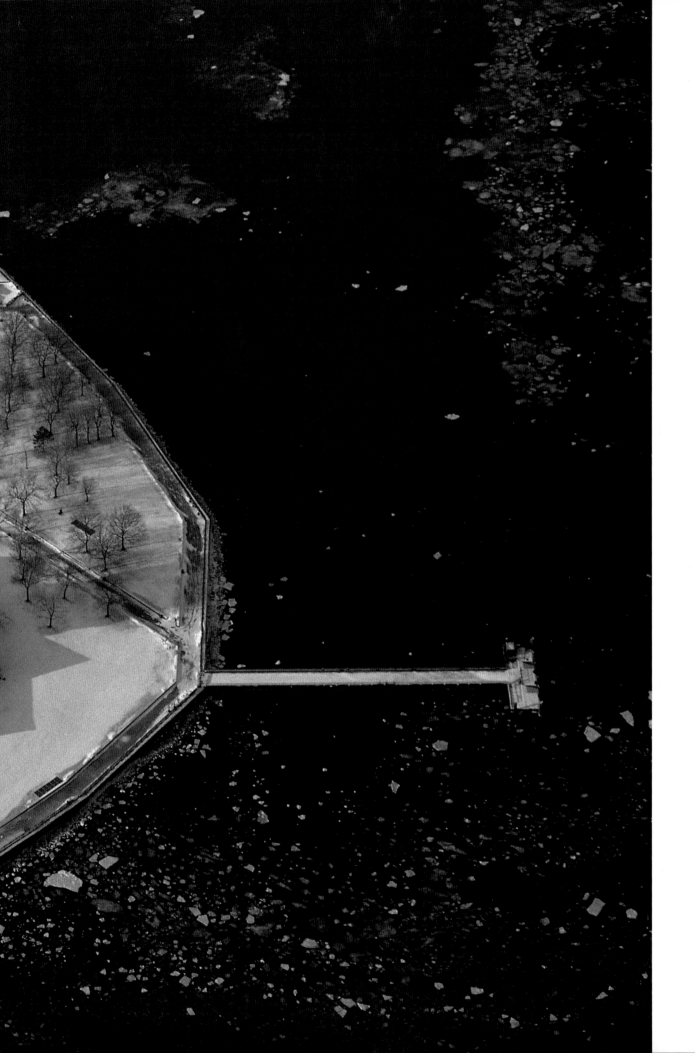

A bare sycamore in front of 17 State Street (1989), by Emery
Roth & Sons

Page 46. Two superheroes do battle in Midtown

Page 47. Jean Dubuffet's *Group of Four Trees* (1972), beneath the Chase Manhattan Bank Tower (1960), by Skidmore, Owings & Merrill

Pages 48–49. *We Shall Beat Our Swords into Plowshares* (1958), by Evgeny Vuchetich, in the United Nations sculpture garden

Page 50. Trash becomes sculpture at Second Street and Avenue B in the East Village

Page 51. The shocking-pink Pandora's Box, one of SoHo's many boutiques

Page 52. The Empire State Building and the New Yorker Hotel, reflected in the Jacob Javits Convention Center (1986), by I.M. Pei

Page 53. Once the tallest and still the most famous building in the world, the Empire State Building (1931), by Shreve, Lamb & Harmon

Page 54. The medal of the French Legion of Honor adorns the top of 29 West 57th Street

Page 55. The Art Deco entrance to the Graybar Building (1927), by Sloan & Robertson

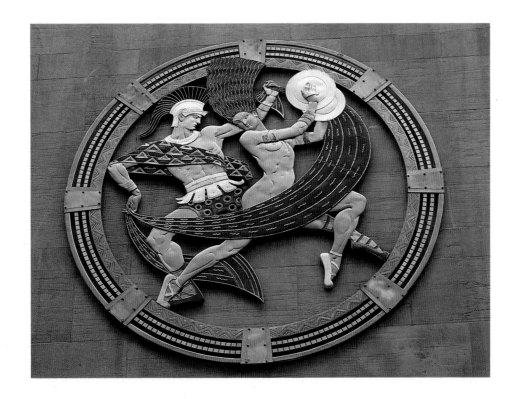

Page 56. The entrances at Rockefeller Center abound with beautiful bas-reliefs, like this one on the GE Building (1933), by Raymond Hood

Page 57. Painted metal reliefs on Radio City Music Hall (1932), by Edward Durrell Stone

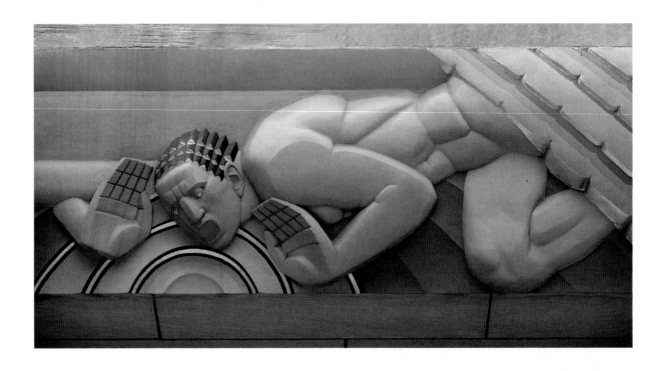

Page 58. Gilded bas-reliefs on the GE Building

Page 59. Carved reliefs depicting industry, above the entrance to 45 Rockefeller Plaza

Pages 60–61. *Prometheus* (1934), by Paul Manship, presides over Rockefeller Center

Page 63. A stylized eagle holds the Box Tree restaurant's sign on East 49th Street

Pages 64–65. The massive and light-filled interior of the Jacob Javits Convention Center, a Crystal Palace on the Hudson River

Page 66. The Beaux Arts facade of the Helmsley Building

Page 67. The Pulitzer Fountain, topped by Karl Bitter's *Pomona*, breathes life into Grand Army Plaza

Page 68. Laundry day in Little Italy

Page 69. A summer art fair takes over the beautiful blocks of lower Fifth Avenue

Page 70. Bergdorf Goodman, the upscale New York shopping mainstay, bedecked with wreaths for Christmas

Page 71. Saks Fifth Avenue, famous for luxurious clothes and personal service

Pages 72–73. Its harbor and rivers frozen in the severe winter of 1984, Manhattan stretches north from the Battery; Battery Park City, at lower left, was just beginning construction

Page 74. The Crown Building (1921), by Warren and Wetmore

Page 75. Skyscrapers old and new near Madison Square: from left, the Metropolitan Life Tower (1909), by Napoleon LeBrun & Sons; 41 Madison Avenue (1972); and the New York Life Building (1928), by Cass Gilbert, with its gilded pyramid

Page 76. The unmistakable triangular Flatiron Building (1902), by Daniel H. Burnham & Co.

Page 77. The afternoon light is caught by the curved wall of 17 State Street above Battery Park

Page 79. A spiderweb of cables flanks the Brooklyn Bridge pedestrian path

Pages 80–81. The sumptuous lobby of the Mayfair Hotel

Page 82. The bright stone-and-copper Croatian Church of St. Cyril and Methodius on West 41st Street

Page 83. The cemetery of Trinity Church, a peaceful downtown oasis; at rear is the American Stock Exchange (1930), by Starrett and Van Vleck

Pages 84–85. An impromptu performance in Washington Square Park, the hub of Greenwich Village

Page 86. A game of sidewalk chess on Mulberry Street in Little Italy

Page 87. Afternoon relaxation outside a SoHo window

Page 88. Preaching on Wall Street next to George Washington

Page 89. A woman pauses to listen to a sidewalk trio in Midtown

Pages 90–91. Rutgers University's famous tuba band, part of Rockefeller Center's annual Christmas celebration

Pages 92–93. The Luna restaurant on Mulberry Street, one of Little Italy's many fine eateries

A freshly restored loft building, ready for a new generation
of tenants

Page 96. Closed shops on 42nd Street get a bright beautification treatment

Page 97. A new mural is painted on East Houston Street

Page 98. The Midtown skyline and Central Park, seen from a restaurant perched high above the park

Page 99. A converted carriage house on 19th Street's "Block Beautiful"

Page 100. The stately entrance to a Midtown townhouse

Page 101. The IBM Building atrium (1983), by Edward Larrabee Barnes, a welcome sea of green on Madison Avenue

Page 102. Early spring flowers bloom in Central Park near Fifth Avenue

Page 103. The peaceful gardens at St. Bartholemew's Church on Park Avenue

Pages 104–5. Dean & Deluca in SoHo, a mecca for gourmets

Page 107. The lighted south Midtown skyline: from left, the Empire State Building, the Metropolitan Life Tower, and the Consolidated Edison Tower

Pages 108–9. The four-star Le Cirque restaurant, a high point of Manhattan cuisine for twenty years

Page 110. Originally private mansions, these brownstones now serve as the entrance to the Helmsley Palace Hotel on Madison Avenue

Page 111. Radio City Music Hall seen above the Exxon Building fountain

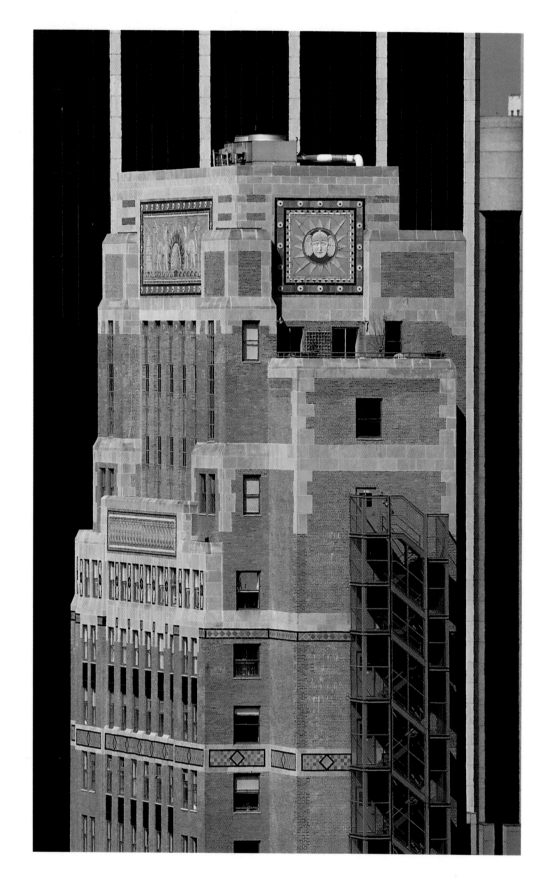

Page 112. The afternoon light catches a hundred-foot-tall mural above 23rd Street

Page 113. Multicolored tile adorns the top of the Fred F. French Building (1927), by H. Douglas Ives and Sloan & Robertson

Pages 114–15. Window washers six hundred feet above Midtown

The Empire State Building, looking northwest toward Midtown

Top. Umberto's Clam House, a Little Italy fixture

Bottom. A Venetian gondola on the Lake in Central Park

Top. A carriage ride through Central Park on a crisp winter day

Bottom. Basketball practice in front of a colorful playground mural in Harlem

Page 120. A medieval statue at the Cloisters, the Metropolitan Museum of Art's reconstruction of a European monastery in upper Manhattan

Page 121. On Fifth Avenue across from St. Patrick's Cathedral (1878), by James Renwick, Jr., Rockefeller Center's *Atlas* holds up the world

Pages 122–23. A fish-eye view of the spiraling interior of the Guggenheim Museum (1959), by Frank Lloyd Wright

Page 124. The Crown Building at night

Page 125. The Metropolitan Life Tower

Pages 126–27. A black-tie party at the Temple of Dendur in the Metropolitan Museum of Art

Page 129. Rush-hour traffic speeds through Columbus Circle and along Broadway and Central Park West

Pages 130–31. On a rainy night, Broadway becomes a mirror for the bright lights of Times Square

Pages 132–33. Moonrise over Manhattan

Rockefeller Center's Christmas tree sparkles above the skating rink

The flower-lined Promenade at Rockefeller Center

In Central Park, spring's cherry blossoms (top) and yellow forsythia (bottom)

A traveler rests at the *Pilgrim Memorial* (1885), by John Quincy Adams Ward

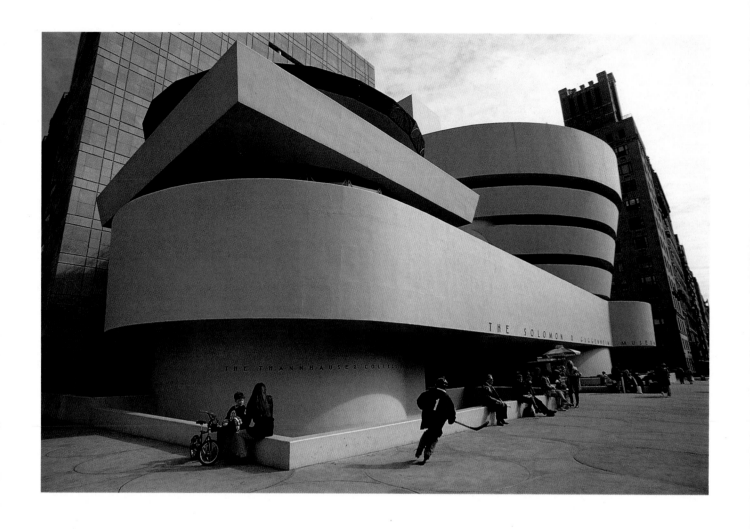

Pages 138–39. Bethesda Fountain, the centerpiece of Frederick Law Olmsted's Central Park

Page 140. Bold geometric shapes define the exterior of Frank Lloyd Wright's Guggenheim Museum

Page 141. The grand facade and fountains of the Metropolitan Museum of Art (1902), by Richard Morris Hunt

Page 143. Gilded gargoyles watch over Midtown at 29 West 57th Street

Page 144. The Stars and Stripes and the Chrysler Building

Page 145. "Patience," one of the stone lions guarding the entrance to the New York Public Library

Page 146. Gapstow Bridge over the Pond in Central Park, a perfect reflecting pool for the Midtown skyline

Page 147. The U.S. Custom House (1907), by Cass Gilbert, one of New York's grandest buildings in the Beaux Arts style, now the Smithsonian Institution's Museum of the American Indian

750 Lexington Avenue (1989), by Murphy/Jahn

Page 149 (top). Some of New York's finest on mounted patrol

Page 149 (bottom). A leather-clad officer at a Central Park ice-skating rink

Pages 150–51. Dusk falls on FDR Drive; in the distance are the Empire State Building and the Midtown skyline, and in the foreground is Bellevue Hospital's New Building

Lower Manhattan from the shipyards of Brooklyn Heights

At left, 909 Third Avenue (1967), by Max O. Urbahn & Associates with
Emery Roth & Sons; at right, the Mondrian (1991), by Fox & Fowle

Pages 154–55. The Brooklyn (foreground) and Manhattan (background) bridges at night

Pages 156–57. Jet fighters on display at the *Intrepid* Sea-Air-Space Museum, a converted World War II aircraft carrier moored on the Hudson River

Page 159. The monumental marble-and-steel lobby of the Empire State Building

Pages 160–61. Sunlight floods the north side of the Museum of Modern Art, redesigned in 1985 by Cesar Pelli

Page 162. Gilded gods recline against the ornate clock of the Helmsley Building

Page 163. A freshly gilded *General William Tecumseh Sherman* (1900), by Augustus Saint-Gaudens, at the southeastern tip of Central Park

TO GENERAL
AM TECUMSEH SHERMAN
BORN FEB 8 1820
DIED FEB 14 1891
BY CITIZENS OF NEW YORK

Georgia O'Keeffe is carried through the art gallery–lined streets of SoHo

Top. *Portrait of a Woman*, c. 1800, by an unknown French painter,
once attributed to Jacques-Louis David, at the Metropolitan
Museum of Art

Bottom. From left, Rembrandt's *Man with a Magnifying Glass*,
Self-portrait, and *Woman with a Pink*, at the Metropolitan
Museum of Art

Page 167. Sidewalk dining in SoHo at I Tre Merli

Page 168. A liveried doorman at Cartier on Fifth Avenue

Page 169. Ivan Chermayeff's large "9" marks the entrance of
9 West 57th Street (1974), by Skidmore, Owings & Merrill

Page 170. A dragon dances in the Chinese New Year's parade in Chinatown

Page 171. A vendor reluctantly parts with his wares in the Flower District

Page 172. The New York City Marathon stretches for miles along Fourth Avenue in Brooklyn

Page 173 (top). The marathon's first leg crosses from Staten Island to Brooklyn on the Verrazano-Narrows Bridge, the longest suspension bridge in North America

Page 173 (bottom). After crossing the marathon's finish line in Central Park, runners wrap themselves in Mylar sheets to retain body heat

Pages 174–75. The frenzied activity of the New York Stock Exchange trading floor

Page 176. Irish police officers proudly march in the St. Patrick's Day Parade

Page 177. A young officer and his friend celebrate St. Patrick's Day

Pages 178–79. A squad of bagpipers leads the St. Patrick's Day Parade up Fifth Avenue

Pages 180–81. Flags of member countries line First Avenue in front of the United Nations General Assembly Building and Headquarters (1947–52), designed by a committee of architects led by Wallace K. Harrison

Page 183. Sailing on the Hudson River

Pages 184, 185, 186–187. The Statue of Liberty (1886), sculpted by Frédéric Auguste Bartholdi and built by Gustave Eiffel, in New York Harbor

Pages 188–89. A cruise ship sails down the Hudson toward the open sea

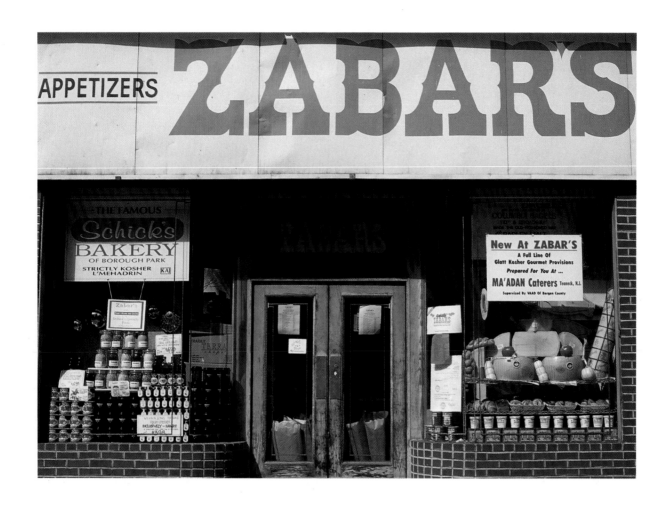

Page 190. Zabar's, the famous Upper West Side gourmet shop, contains wall-to-wall delicacies from around the world

Page 191. The Shrine of St. Elizabeth Ann Seton and its Rectory are lone survivors of the eighteenth century on Battery Park

Page 192. Mansion-like row houses (1890s), by Clarence F. True, along Riverside Drive on the Upper West Side

Page 193. The Cloisters' beautiful gardens are framed by medieval architecture transplanted from Europe

Page 195. In the foreground, the cupola of City Hall (1803–12), by Mangin & McComb, topped by a statue of Justice, and in the background, the Municipal Building (1914), by McKim, Mead and White

Pages 196–97. Southeastern view of Midtown and the East River

Pages 198–99. The Brooklyn Bridge and the Empire State Building, seen from the Brooklyn Heights Promenade

NATIONAL
COLD STORAGE
CO

THE LINCOLN
SAVINGS BANK

HELPING TO REBUILD
A BETTER NEW YORK

Page 200. The Empire State Building, framed by the Manhattan Bridge

Page 201. The Queensboro Bridge and the Roosevelt Island Tram rise above 59th Street

Page 202. A passing gull catches the sunset in front of the World Trade Center

Page 203. The Chrysler Building, the jewel of the Midtown skyline

Pages 204–5. Citicorp Center (1978), by Hugh Stubbins & Associates, points its angled roof skyward; Philip Johnson's oval Lipstick Building (1986) is at right

Pages 206–7. Lower Manhattan and the Brooklyn Bridge at sunset

ACKNOWLEDGMENTS

New York is one of the most photographed cities in the world. For this reason, it is not easy to create yet another book without being redundant or obvious. Even to people who know the city, however, New York is constantly showing new faces—in some parts, the city even looks at itself, great buildings reflecting in the facades of mirrored neighbors across the street.

Thousands of people from hundreds of different nations walk up and down the avenues, making it a truly cosmopolitan place. Exciting store windows with the latest fashions, Rockefeller Center, Central Park, Lincoln Center, SoHo, Chinatown, Wall Street, the Chrysler Building, the Museum of Modern Art, the Metropolitan Museum of Art, the Guggenheim—these are just a few of the features that make New York the center of the world.

As Frank Sinatra sings of New York City, "If I can make it there, I'd make it anywhere"; I made it here, and numerous people helped. Thank you to the New York City Convention and Visitors Bureau for their assistance, to Olympia & York for the use of their rooftops in several locations, and to all the New York City establishments that appear on these pages. This book could not have been done without my publisher, Charles Miers, who believed in the project; my editors, Jen Bilik and Jim Stave; and the designer, Gilda Hannah. I am especially honored to thank Mayor Edward I. Koch, whose eloquent words introduce this book.